Original title:
Yeti or Not, Here Comes Winter

Copyright © 2024 Creative Arts Management OÜ
All rights reserved.

Author: Atticus Thornton
ISBN HARDBACK: 978-9916-94-268-0
ISBN PAPERBACK: 978-9916-94-269-7

Beneath the Blanket of White

Snowflakes dance like tiny bits,
They tumble down, they tease and flit.
Beneath the blanket, cozy, bright,
We laugh and play, what a delight!

Hot cocoa spills on silly mittens,
As snowballs fly, the fun just thickens.
With every slip, a laugh erupts,
In winter's arms, the joy corrupts.

Unseen Mysteries in Winter

What hides beneath the frosty tree?
Is it a creature, wild and free?
Or just a squirrel in a funny hat,
Wearing snow like some wacky brat?

The icicles hang with elegant flair,
Is that a smile or frost-bitten glare?
With whispers of secrets caught in the air,
Winter's mischief is everywhere!

The Frosted Footsteps

Footsteps crunch in the morning chill,
Poking through snowdrifts, such a thrill.
Who made these marks, where might they lead?
Could it be magic, or just a need?

An echo here of laughter clear,
As we chase winter's whimsy near.
Each print a puzzle, quaint and fun,
Unraveling treats before we run!

Ghosts of the Winter Woods

In ghostly woods, the shadows prance,
With every gust, they seem to dance.
Are they just trees dressed up to play,
Or chilly friends who've lost their way?

With giggles echoing through the frost,
We wander deeper, not quite lost.
Every snap and crunch makes us grin,
As winter's secrets draw us in.

Frost's Embrace

Snowflakes dancing in the air,
Tickle my nose without a care.
Sipping cocoa hot and sweet,
Slippers on my icy feet.

Penguins waddle by my door,
Who invited them? What's in store?
Snowmen plotting up a scheme,
Are they plotting? Not a dream.

Days of Ice and Mystery

Chilly breezes swirl around,
Icicles hang, a crystal crown.
Hats and scarves in colors bright,
Fashion faux pas? What a sight!

Sledding down the snowy hill,
Laughing till we get our fill.
Mittens lost, oh what a quest,
Winter's chill, but we jest!

The Shivers Beneath the Stars

Under blankets, we all huddle,
Chasing giggles, avoiding the puddle.
Snowflakes whisper soft and low,
What secrets do they know?

Hot pot dinners, a warming feast,
Family tales from west to east.
The stars above, all shiny bright,
Tell us stories every night.

Midwinter Murmurs

Frosty mornings make me shiver,
Tickle fights make spirits quiver.
Snowball fights, who will win?
Laughter echoes, let's begin!

Frozen noses, rosy cheeks,
We're all tipsy from the peaks.
Winter fun, a wild spree,
Wrap me in your mystery!

Echoes of the Snowy Expanse

In the frosty fields, we prance,
Chasing shadows that weave and dance.
Snowflakes tickle, make us giggle,
Watch us slip, oh what a wiggle!

Snowmen towering, hats askew,
Juggling carrots, what a view!
Sleds that spin with whoops and laughs,
Winter's joy in silly drafts.

Hushed Stories Beneath the Snow

Silent whispers from the trees,
Snowflakes falling with the breeze.
Frosty mittens, noses red,
Tales of pranks, where snowballs wed.

Beneath the cover, critters hide,
Wearing scarves, and boots with pride.
Together we share a silly tale,
Of frozen toes and snowball hail!

The Glacial Veil

A glacial veil draped o'er the hill,
With giggles echoing, such a thrill!
Lavish laughter fills the air,
As the snowmen dance without a care.

Squirrels in hats, plotting their schemes,
Catch the snowflakes slipping through dreams.
With a wink and a nudge, they spin about,
In this winter wonder, there's no doubt!

Secrets of the Frigid Night

Underneath the moon so bright,
Laughter bubbles in the night.
Snowball fights and secret plans,
Prancing reindeer, jolly bands.

Starlit jokes and cheerful fun,
Chasing shadows just for a run.
With frosty breath and hearts aglow,
We whisper tales only snowflakes know!

The Wintry Wraith

In the frosty air, a ghostly sight,
Dancing shadows in the pale moonlight.
Misplaced mittens, where are they now?
A ghostly laugh, 'Oh, look at me plow!'

Snowflakes twirl like a mad ballet,
While snowmen wobble and then decay.
A whispering chill, what's that I see?
Just a prankster dressed in white, oh me!

A Tale of Winter's Shadows

Snowball fights with laughter resound,
But wait, what's lurking all around?
A broomstick flying, oh what a scene,
Mischief managed by a squirrel, so keen!

Hats that fly off in the frosty breeze,
Haunted by snowflakes that tease,
Chasing a rogue scarf, oh what a twist,
Winter fun, you surely can't miss!

Footprints of the Unknown

These strange tracks lead to who knows where,
Could it be a bear or a circus bear pair?
Puddles of snow, a curious plight,
A giggle escapes, as I take flight!

With every step in the white powdery sea,
I imagine the creatures, wild and free.
Pigeon or penguin? What will they wear?
I'll take a photo, if they don't glare!

Whispers in the Snowstorm

Whispers flying like confetti in air,
Snowflakes giggle, without a care.
What's that sound? Is it a tune?
An avalanche of laughter beneath the moon!

Frosty beards packed with snow so white,
Icicles hanging, what a silly sight!
Sledding down hills with a squeal and shout,
Winter, oh winter, you bring such clout!

Beneath the Veil of Snowflakes

Snowflakes dance with glee,
In a flurry that won't freeze.
The world's a white, soft bed,
Where penguins laugh instead.

Hot chocolate's on the stove,
Marshmallows dive, they grove.
While polar bears make snowmen,
And giggle once and again.

Frosty Tales from the Northern Depths

Elk order drinks on ice,
While rabbits roll the dice.
A moose with shades so cool,
Thinks hockey is the rule.

Snowmen gossip and share
The latest winter flair.
With carrots looking sly,
They wink and say, "Oh my!"

The Winter Whisperers

Frosty breezes tell a tale,
Of penguins sweeping trails.
They slip and slide with flair,
While snowflakes toss in air.

Squirrels sew their cozy hats,
While raccoons chat with bats.
A chorus of chittering sounds,
In snowy joy, all around.

Snow Shadows and Superstitions

Whispers in the winter night,
Of shadows dancing light.
They claim they saw a bear,
In pajamas, unaware!

A snowball war ensues,
With frosty epic views.
And yetis, hiding so sly,
Watch from the trees up high!

Beneath the Winter's Cloak

Snowflakes dance in the chilly air,
Sleds go flying without a care.
Snowmen wobble, carrots askew,
They're plotting a snowball war, who knew?

Hot cocoa spills on mittens bright,
Giggling children in pure delight.
Icicles dangle like teeth on a smile,
Winter's charm holds us for a while.

Glimpses of the Frozen Unknown

In frosty breath, we tell our tales,
Of slippery paths and snowy trails.
Yet what lurks beneath this cold veneer,
Are mischief-makers, we should all fear!

A scarf strewn over, a hat in flight,
It's chaos when life's a snowball fight.
Frozen noses poke through frosty seams,
We giggle at the snow's silly schemes.

An Evening with the Winter Spirits

Candles flicker in the snowy night,
We hear the whispers of winter's bite.
Are they spirits or just foxes in the snow?
Chasing shadows, they put on a show!

With every gust, the doors creak wide,
Ghostly giggles join us for the ride.
They dance around with a mischievous glee,
Turning snowflakes into a winter spree.

Frost-Kissed Anxieties

Oh frost, you tease with your crispy breath,
While we loiter, pondering our own death!
One slip on ice, and off we go,
Laughing at the tumbles, putting on a show.

Scarves strangling necks, boots with flair,
Winding through snow like we haven't a care.
Yet underneath our bright, cheerful grins,
Lies the dread of where the autumn's been!

Shadows in the Snowdrift

In the moonlight, shadows play,
Hiding creatures on display,
Skis and boots just left behind,
What could be lurking, oh so blind?

Fluffy tails and snowy paws,
Peer from mounds without a pause,
A snowball fight, a thud, a squall,
Was it fun or did we fall?

Laughter echoes through the night,
While snowmen stand, a funny sight,
A creature giggles, can you hear?
Or was that just a passing deer?

The snowman wears a funny hat,
With carrots and a silly spat,
But wait, is that a hand or claw?
A snowball fight, oh what a draw!

When Winter Calls the Unseen

Whispers glide through frosty air,
Rumors fly without a care,
Footprints lead where none should go,
In the snow, they twist and flow.

A giant sneeze, the snowflakes swirl,
Laughter roars, as tales unfurl,
Three snowmen in a snowball clash,
Who's hiding there? Aw, just a stash!

Hot cocoa spills, giggles abound,
In the chill, the warmth is found,
What dances near the icy pine?
A mystery wrapped in winter's shine!

Snowflakes twirl and tumble down,
Comedy reigns as giggles drown,
Are they dancing, or is that me?
Winter's show, a comedy spree!

The Tundra's Silent Watcher

In the tundra, whispers sigh,
Something's watching from nearby,
With a giggle and a skip,
The nature of our funny trip.

Puffballs wobble, roll around,
Fluffy friends beneath the ground,
What's that peeking through the drift?
Ah, a snowball makes a swift gift!

Overhead, the skies are clear,
While down below, we sense our fear,
But laughter echoes, breaks the cold,
With stories funny, never old.

Tundra secrets, oh so sly,
Underneath the frosty sky,
A snicker here, a chuckle there,
An unseen friend, we know they care!

Glacial Mysteries at Dusk

As day fades into winter's hush,
Laughter stirs in a warming rush,
Why did the snowman wear a frown?
Looks like winter's turned him down!

In shadows cast by fading light,
Silly creatures stretch and bite,
Their snowball antics, fast and bright,
Who knew ice could feel so light?

Chill in the air, yet warmth inside,
A chilly friend, a laughing guide,
Mysteries of the night unfold,
As winter tales are spun and told.

Glimpses of fun beneath the stars,
Echo laughter from afar,
In winter's heart, we dance and play,
With glacial mysteries on display!

Legends Wrapped in Snow

In the mountains, tales do grow,
Of creatures in the winter's glow.
They dance around, they leap and bound,
In fluffy coats they're seldom found.

With snowballs tossed like playful jests,
They hide in woods, they pad the rests.
But once the sun begins to fade,
The legends laugh, their paths well laid.

The Enigma of the Winter Wilderness

In frosty air, a riddle brews,
With flappy feet and fuzzy shoes.
Tracks in snow that twist and swerve,
Leave us guessing where they serve.

Hot cocoa sips, we sit and squint,
At shadows dancing in the glint.
Could it be? A furry king?
Or just a dog with flair? We sing!

Shadows Creeping in the Snowfall

Beneath the flakes, what's lurking near?
A big ol' tease, or just a deer?
With every crunch, we leap and spin,
In cotton white, let games begin!

Whispers swirl of cuddly fright,
In snowy mists, they play all night.
But all we find are prints so cute,
Perhaps a bear in fuzzy boots?

Arctic Echoes

In frosty woods, they start to hum,
With clumsy moves, they play and drum.
They twirl in snow, all goofy grace,
Unseen, they leave a chilly trace.

While we sip soup, they make a fuss,
In hidden glades, they giggle thus.
The arctic air holds secrets tight,
But we just laugh, it's pure delight.

Echoes in the Icy Silence

Snowflakes dance in a clumsy way,
They giggle and tumble, then fade away.
A snowman winks with his carrot nose,
As he dreams of melting in warmer prose.

Penguins slide with a comical grace,
Toppling over in a snowy race.
Ski tracks zigzag, turn into a mess,
Who knew winter could bring such distress?

Hot cocoa spills from a mug in haste,
Marshmallows float like a sweet little waste.
Frosty giggles fill the chilly air,
While squirrels chatter without a care.

Laughter echoes in the crisp, cold night,
As snowballs fly with unmeasured might.
Winter may be a frosty foe,
But fun awaits in the winter's glow.

Chilling Spirits on the Slopes

Slippers on sleds, what a strange sight,
As kids scream joyfully down the height.
A tumble here, a flip or two,
Chilly cheeks painted in shades of blue.

Snowmen dance with a cartwheel spin,
Their twiggy arms making snowball wins.
Giggling ghosts roam the frozen ground,
Haunting the hills with a frosty sound.

A flamingo on skis, quite bizarre,
Sliding with flair, a true winter star.
A dog in a cape fetches his ball,
Bounding through snowdrifts, oh what a thrall!

Chilling spirits in hats so tall,
Watch as winter plays with us all.
With laughter, gingerbread, and cheer,
This season of fun is finally here!

Frosted Folklore Amidst the Pines

A slippery tale through the pine trees,
Whispers of squirrels and cheeky bees.
Legends of laughter travel the night,
As icicles twinkle with pure delight.

A dragon in mittens, a sight so rare,
Breathes clouds of giggles in the frosty air.
Reindeer on roller skates zoom by,
Chasing their shadows beneath the sky.

Fables unfold with a shimmy and shake,
As snowball fights leave a sparkly wake.
With each frosty breath, new stories bloom,
In the heart of winter's frozen room.

Warmth in the chill makes our hearts sing,
In this frosted realm, it's a magical thing.
So grab your snow boots, let's take a ride,
On this whimsical journey, let's not hide!

The Howl of the Wintry Wilderness

The wind howls tunes of a jolly tune,
As snowflakes join in, a wintry boon.
Creatures in coats bounce all around,
Exploring the snow-covered, glistening ground.

A moose in a scarf struts with delight,
While beavers build bridges each snowy night.
Snow bunnies hop with a rhythm divine,
Hopping and squeaking, oh how they shine!

Frosty footprints dance in the glow,
As we join the frolic in the moon's show.
Chasing shadows in this wintery maze,
With tickles of frost and laughter ablaze.

So let's embrace the howls of the night,
With stories and giggles, pure, shining light.
In this frosty tapestry, we all play a part,
As winter's joy spills into every heart.

Frost-Blanketed Secrets

Under blankets of frosty white,
Hiding secrets, oh what a sight!
Penguins pranksters slip and slide,
Snowmen giggle, filled with pride.

Icicles dangle, like teeth of doom,
Yet they're just hanging out in gloom.
A bunny hops with a winking eye,
"Catch me if you can!" it dares to fly.

Snowflakes dance, a flurry of cheer,
Spreading joy and winter's sneer.
Elves on sleds race downhill,
Each tumble sparkles, a zany thrill.

With mittens lost and scarves unruly,
Sledding turns to snowball folly.
Laughter rings in the crisp cold air,
Winter's mischief everywhere!

Specters of the Snowbound Hills

Hills of white, a ghostly scene,
Where snowmen whisper, quiet and lean.
Yet here they twirl, in a wacky dance,
Bouncing like they've taken a chance.

Amidst the trees, with grins so wide,
Frosty figures take a ride.
Snowflakes winking, tricks on the way,
Gliding down on a sleigh of hay.

A snowdrift's end, a bunny's nest,
Chortling critters put to the test.
A snowball fight ensues in glee,
"Missed me!" shouts one, full of esprit.

Over the hills, what a ruckus bright,
Chasing shadows, day turns to night.
In this snowy realm, laughter rings clear,
Specters of fun, winter's cavalier.

A Dance of Winter Spirits

Out in the cold, a flicker of fun,
Winter spirits dance, everyone's spun.
Twisting and twirling in the chilly air,
Spreading laughter everywhere!

Snowflakes shimmer like tiny jewels,
Goblins break all of winter's rules.
Socks on snowboards dash with glee,
Who knew this could be so silly?

They gather 'round an icy pond,
Waiting for a slip, a laugh to respond.
Frosty faces, cheeks aglow,
Sipping cocoa, stealing the show!

With a giggle and a jolly shout,
Who needs warmth when you have this clout?
These winter spirits bring such delight,
Dancing their way through snowy night.

Frost's Intriguing Enigma

Frost creeps in with giggles and sighs,
Turning rooftops into icy pies.
What's hidden beneath this chilly ruse?
A snowman's top hat? The latest muse?

Icicles wink from rooftops so high,
Challenging children to give it a try.
Some slip and tumble with comical flair,
While others just giggle, avoiding despair.

Snow angels flapping their frosty wings,
Sculpting laughter, oh what joy it brings.
Caught in the moment, they break into cheer,
In winter's embrace, there's nothing to fear!

So join the ruckus, don't be shy,
Frost's enigma calls you to fly!
With snowflakes dancing all around,
A winter wonderland, joy abounds!

The Enigma of the First Snow.

A flurry falls, the world's aglow,
Cats jump high, and dogs just know.
Snowflakes swirling all around,
Laughter echoes, joy is found.

Mittens lost and hats on heads,
Sleds go flying, adults like kids.
Hot cocoa spills on winter coats,
Snowmen's noses made from oats.

Down the street, a snowball flies,
In the air, surprise and sighs.
Frosty beards on cheeks so red,
Giggles sound, no tears to shed.

Icicles hang like chandelier,
Winter's here, let's all cheer!
With scarves wrapped tight, we dance and prance,
In this chill, we take a chance.

Snowbound Shadows

The shadows stretch beneath the trees,
A playful chill blows through the leaves.
Snowballs bounce off windows wide,
As laughter echoes, joy can't hide.

Sleds collide, and someone slips,
We're all wrapped up in winter's grip.
Snowmen wink with carrot smiles,
Snowball fights go on for miles.

Yet what lurks behind those drifts?
Alas, the mystery of snowman's gifts!
With eyes that sparkle, snowflakes twirl,
Frolicking kids in a winter whirl.

Midnight comes, the shadows creep,
In the snow, the secrets keep.
With laughs and jokes, we share a glance,
In winter's arms, we take our stance.

Frosty Footprints

Footprints crunch in fresh white snow,
Who made these tracks? We want to know!
Each step holds a story, a grin,
Let the adventures now begin!

Penguins slide, and children chase,
Frosty breath in this icy race.
Snowmen wave as we march by,
And snowflakes twinkle from the sky.

A puppy bounds, a cat retreats,
In this chill, it's fun that beats.
With frosty noses, we explore,
Dancing through the winter's door.

Hot chocolate dreams at the day's end,
With marshmallows, our laughter blends.
These frosty footprints lead us home,
In this snowy world, we happily roam.

Whispering Winds of December

The December winds begin to play,
Whispering secrets at the end of day.
Snowflakes dance in a twinkling trance,
A chilly air that dares us to prance.

Scarves wrap tight, and cheeks turn pink,
In the frosty air, we start to think.
A snowball fight ignites the fun,
As laughter rolls beneath the sun.

Twinkling lights adorn each street,
Winter wonderlands are hard to beat.
Hopeful hearts in a snowflakes' drift,
In every flake, we find a gift.

So let us frolic, let us jest,
In this chilly chill, we feel so blessed.
With winter's magic, let's gather round,
For joy and laughter in snow abound.

The Creature of the Cold

In a coat of fluffy white,
The creature dances with delight.
Furry arms and lashed-on mittens,
Is it a monster? No, it's just kittens!

Snowballs flying through the air,
Dodging flurries without a care.
Underneath a thick white shroud,
That giggling sound? Oh, it's just loud!

Chasing shadows, making trails,
Carving laughter, never fails.
With a twirl and goofy spin,
Who knew snow could hold such din?

So if you hear a funny thump,
And see some fluff lead to a jump,
Just smile wide, don't be too bold,
It's simply the creature of the cold!

In the Heart of the Frozen Forest

Deep in woods where snowflakes fall,
Lives a critter, oh so small.
With a hat so big, it flops and flares,
His wiggle dance brings snowflake stares!

Bumping trees, leaving tracks,
Singing tunes that get no slack.
Rolling in the powdery fluff,
He's a snowy goof, and that's no bluff!

Under branches, slyly peeks,
With icicle fangs, he slyly squeaks.
Watch him trip in cozy snow,
Creating sparkles in a blow!

Giggles echo through the trees,
He's a jolly rascal, the cold breeze.
So tiptoe gently, join his fun,
In the frozen forest, joy's begun!

Silent Pathways of the Icebound

On silent paths, where shadows creep,
Skates on ice, not a peep.
Footprints left, in shapes that baffle,
Who carved these? They must be daft-ful!

Laughter rings, as they glide near,
Slipping, sliding, full of cheer.
With stumble and giggle, a big ol' flop,
The chilly air, we won't stop!

Snowmen stand in poses bold,
Each one's face is just pure gold.
With a carrot nose and coal for eyes,
These frosty friends just love to rise!

So if you wander where it's bright,
Follow the laughter into night.
The pathways gleam with fun and glee,
Evolving winter's jubilee!

Dreaming in a Snowy Realm

In dreams of snow, the world's so bright,
Imagining creatures in playful flight.
Mittens tossed on the frosty ground,
The laughter of friends is the sweetest sound.

Snowflakes swirl with a dizzy grace,
Chasing shadows, it's a silly race.
Twirling around in a sleepy haze,
Who knew winter brought such playful days?

Pajamas snug, hot cocoa near,
As tale-tellers search for things we cheer.
Whispers of snowmen in the night,
Made of dreams, it just feels right!

So let's all dream in this snowy swath,
Of creatures cuddled in frosty cloth.
A realm of laughter, simple bliss,
Where winter magic is hard to miss!

Tracks in the Gleaming Snow

In the glow of frosty light,
Something danced out of sight.
Could it be a furry friend,
Or a prank that just won't end?

Footprints dash and leave a trail,
A chase of snowflakes in the gale.
Was that laughter in the breeze?
Or just squirrels playing tease?

Snowmen wear a puzzled grin,
As they watch the fun begin.
With a carrot top and stick in hand,
Could they too make a funny stand?

So if you see a shadow pass,
Don't forget to wear your sass.
For if the snow begins to play,
Join the fun, don't shy away!

Frosty Fables of the North

Tall tales wrap in snowflakes white,
Like a dog who took a flight.
Chasing tails through snowy piles,
Leaving trails and fuzzy smiles.

A bear with a scarf too snug,
Trying to give a moose a hug.
Both tangled in winter's lace,
Laughter echoing in this space.

An owl hoots a frosty pun,
As chipmunks race just for fun.
With acorn hats and snowball wars,
The forest bursts with winter scores.

Each frosty tale has its twist,
In snowball fights, they can't resist.
This season's here, just let it flow,
With giggles wrapped in frosty glow!

The Mysterious Chill of Nightfall

When darkness falls, the chill arrives,
Where magic stirs and laughter thrives.
A snowflake giggles as it flies,
While frost nips noses; hear the sighs.

Beneath the stars, a shadow slinks,
Is it a ghost or just a wink?
Jack Frost tries to play a game,
While everyone just calls his name.

Whispers float through icy air,
Of snowball schemes and playful flair.
With chilly fingers and frosty toes,
Who's out there? Just winter, it shows!

The night plays tricks with every sound,
As laughter dances all around.
So snuggle in for cozy fun,
The night's not over, there's just begun!

Whispers of the Winter Wild

Windswept whispers fill the pines,
Echoing tales in twisted lines.
Creatures stir with crafty grins,
Plotting mischief in their skins.

A rabbit hops with dapper style,
Sporting boots that make us smile.
While fox twirls in a snowy swirl,
Winter's fun, they give a twirl.

The moon peeks in with a bright beam,
Spotting all their frosty schemes.
Snowflakes giggle as they swirl,
In this winter, let dreams unfurl.

For in this wild, the fun won't cease,
With every paw and snowy fleece.
Join the dance, the night is right,
With giggles hidden from the light!

The Hidden Beings of the Frost

In the chill of the night, they sneak,
With a giggle and a hefty squeak.
Snowmen wobble, giving a fright,
As the snowballs take wing in their flight.

Under moonlight, the shadows play,
Whispering secrets in their frosty way.
With snickers and dustings of snow,
They slide down the hills, all aglow.

Beans and snowflakes, an odd little crew,
Each winter, they come, and the silliness grew.
Dancing and tumbling in white shiny coats,
While sleds zoom by with laughter that floats.

In the flurry of flakes, a parade takes form,
With puppets and giggles, they weather the storm.
As we sip hot chocolate, with marshmallows twice,
We wonder if there's room for a slice of their spice.

Beneath the Storm of Snow

Beneath the wide sky, clouds start to rumble,
As tiny snow creatures giggle and tumble.
They craft their own forts, with towers of fluff,
And laugh at the world when the weather gets tough.

Chasing each other, they slip and they slide,
Making snow angels with arms open wide.
In the swirl of the blizzard, a snowball goes whizzing,
And everyone knows, it's all about frizzing!

Tales of mischief, they spread like warm cheer,
As frost-covered friends find their way to appear.
Just wait till the morning, when sunlight shall glow,
You'll see all their antics in a bright, sparkly show.

Under the laughter, the whispers take flight,
As they peek from behind every frosty white height.
Oh, what a surprise, when they all come to play,
In the heart of the storm, there's fun going your way!

Nightfall and the Winter Spirits

When night falls low, and the stars start to twinkle,
In the frosty air, you might hear a crinkle.
The winter spirits sprout from their slumber,
With bubbling giggles that fill up the lumber.

Snowflakes descend like a playful brigade,
Tickling your nose, in a fluffy parade.
They toss little snowballs and dash out of sight,
Leaving laughter and whispers within the moonlight.

Chortles and chuckles dance in the breeze,
While icicles shimmer on the branches of trees.
Beneath the wonder of the chilly night air,
The spirits are playing without any care.

So if you hear laughter or see a swift flash,
Know it's just winter's impromptu, joyful bash.
Beneath the cold cover, there's magic alive,
In every snowflake, the giggles survive!

Echoes Across the Icy Expanse

Across the vast fields, the echoes roll wide,
With bursts of bright laughter that can't be denied.
As ice critters gather to have a big ball,
The merriment tumbles, just hear the call!

In the crisp winter air, their antics resound,
With snowmen all waltzing, spinning around.
They sing silly songs, in the freshness of white,
While they duck and they doddle, a magical sight!

Through the cold of the night, the echoes ripple,
As snowflakes take turns in a playful tipple.
With frozen confetti that glitters and glows,
The charm of the winter, a joyous show grows.

So dance with the frost, let your laughter flow free,
For the season brings cheer, just like a warm tea.
In the echoing silence, hear all the fun,
For under the frost, the spirits all run!

Frosty Myths Under the Moonlight

In the woods where shadows play,
A creature stalks, or so they say.
With a belly full of snowflake treats,
It dances gleefully on frozen streets.

Snowball fights with a frosty friend,
Chasing him, I thought it'd end.
But the round man just rolls away,
He laughs, then hides 'til break of day.

Under moons of silver light,
The whispers of the chill ignite.
Are they stories, or truth untold?
Watching secrets in the cold.

Neighbors claim last year they saw,
A fuzzy beast with toothy jaw.
But when they peeked, just a pile of snow,
With a scarf and boots, what a funny show!

Shadows in the Snowdrifts

Bigfoot's cousin made a stop,
With a belly flop, he made a plop.
While kids make angels, he's making fun,
Sneaking snacks, he's never done!

Footprints lead to nowhere fast,
Buried snacks from seasons past.
What's hidden deep in white so bright?
A stash of treats, oh what a sight!

The snowdrifts hide delightful clues,
Of fuzzy socks and mismatched shoes.
We chase the giggles, all around,
In the drifting laughter, joy is found.

But wait, a snowball flies so high,
Dunked right in his frosty pie!
The beast just shrugs and takes a bite,
In shadows where the snowflakes light.

Legends of the Frostbitten Peaks

On peaks so high, they say it's true,
A giant sneezed and made a brew.
Hot cocoa spilled, the world drank deep,
Snowy tales we'd all keep.

They say he bumbles, trips, and falls,
Then builds a fortress from frozen walls.
But watch your step, he left a treat,
A cocoa-scented, snowman feat!

Popcorn garlands, on trees they cling,
Frosty giggles, the legends sing.
With every step, a crunch, a cheer,
As stories twist into the year.

So raise your mugs and laugh out loud,
To winter's tales, we are allowed.
Dance in snow and let joy peak,
For frosty legends are what we seek!

The Snowman's Secret

Once a snowman, tall and bright,
Held a secret, out of sight.
In his carrot nose, a joke was wed,
He'd quip and giggle when folks were fed.

With button eyes that glimmered keen,
He'd wink and chuckle without being seen.
While kids were busy at play with glee,
He'd steal their mittens, oh what a spree!

The kids all wondered where they went,
As he cuddled them, all content.
In snowball fights, he'd join the fray,
With frosty hugs throughout the play!

So when you build your friend in snow,
Just know his humor's on the go.
With every flake that melts to ground,
His silly spirit will be found!

Frosted Trails of the Unknown

In the woods where snowflakes dance,
A creature lurks, perhaps by chance.
With fuzzy feet and a silly grin,
He trips on ice, let the fun begin!

His breath makes clouds, a frosty delight,
He giggles loud, what a strange sight!
With a hat made of pine and a scarf of grey,
He rolls in the snow, oh what a play!

A snowball fight, he shouts, 'not fair!'
They laugh and dodge without a care.
Belly flops and snow angels abound,
The happiest creature you've ever found!

As night falls down, he winks with glee,
Hiding in shadows, not hard to see.
He yodels a tune that brings the cheer,
Oh, winter fun, come experience here!

Secrets Entombed in Snow

Beneath the fluff of snowy blankets,
Lies a secret opposite of the fanket.
A jolly beast with a belly so round,
In a frozen lake, he's tumble-bound!

He wears a coat of twinkling frost,
When he slips, he laughs, 'What a cost!'
Chasing snowflakes, he leaps and he bounds,
In his snowy realm, pure fun abounds!

He stops for a snack of ice cream chill,
Meets a squirrel who's got quite the skill.
With a dance-off challenge, they twirl and spin,
In the glowing moonlight, let the games begin!

They build a fort for the next big play,
Where snowy figures cheerfully sway.
Secrets lurk in the shimmering glow,
Come join the fun, where the laughter grows!

Frostbitten Adventures

An icy breeze and a hat askew,
Adventure calls in a wintery hue.
With slippery slopes, our hero dives,
He summersaults, oh, how he thrives!

Down the hill he rolls with glee,
The world's a snow-capped jubilee.
With a crooked smile and frozen toes,
He spins like a top, then over he goes!

His friends all gather, they can't miss this,
A winter party that's pure bliss.
With marshmallow hats and cocoa cups,
They dance around until the sun erupts!

At day's end, they sit and sip,
Laughing hard, they let it rip.
Frostbitten tales of joy and cheer,
Winter's embrace, let's persevere!

Whispers of the Winter Veil

The snowflakes fall like whispered dreams,
Each caught on tongues, like silly beams.
A frosty fellow, with a shivery laugh,
Takes a slide on his big, puffy calf!

He calls out, 'Catch me if you can!'
As he zooms past the wobbly man.
With all his friends in a snowball splat,
They giggle and roll, oh, look at that!

They build a snowman with marshmallow treats,
A nose of carrot and candy feats.
With scarves around those frosty necks,
The joy echoes, what fun-expect!

As the evening falls, the stars appear,
The air is crisp, laughter's near.
Whispers of joy and frosty fun,
Winter's secrets, the night has begun!

Chilling Tales from the Ice

In frosty nights when shadows play,
Snowmen have their secret sway.
With carrot noses pointing high,
They giggle softly, oh my, oh my!

Polar bears in woolly hats,
Sipping cocoa with their cats.
Penguins slide on toast with glee,
All while plotting a grand jubilee!

Icicles hang like winter's claws,
While snowflakes dance with muffled applause.
The frozen lake hides a playful show,
Where frosty friends put on their glow!

So gather 'round, let laughter ring,
As frostbitten tales of fun we bring.
In the chill, let joy ignite,
There's mischief brewing all through the night!

The Silent Stalker Beneath the Snow

Through the snow, a crunch, a slide,
Look out, there's magic far and wide!
With furry feet and playful eyes,
A fluffy ghost in disguise!

Beneath the drifts, a merry prank,
Sleds are waiting, no time to tank!
With every jump, a poof, a puff,
Who knew the magic was this tough?

Whispers carried on the breeze,
Raccoons chuckling in the trees.
They scurry 'round with merry cheer,
While winter grins, "I'm glad you're here!"

Oh, frigid air and frosty light,
Laughter twinkles through the night.
So cozy up and take a look,
At winter's secret storybook!

Elusive Beasts of the Frozen Realm

In snow-clad woods where shadows creep,
Elusive beasts awake from sleep.
Fluffy tails and bells that jingle,
They prance around feet as they mingle.

The hare hops high with shoes of flair,
While sly foxes toss snow in the air.
With every leap and joyful glance,
They choreograph a winter dance!

But what's this sound? A muffled roar,
Is it a bear or something more?
With furry hats and twinkling eyes,
They hide beneath the snowy skies.

Oh, frosty friends and giggly yells,
Winter's secrets are full of spells.
Join the fun, let laughter bloom,
For winter's here to fill the room!

Winter's Hidden Wanderer

Who roams the hills when frost is near?
A mystic figure filled with cheer.
With puffy boots and stylish flair,
They leave behind a giggling air.

Flakes swirl round in a wild race,
As snowballs fly through chilly space.
But watch your back with a playful glance,
For winter's tricks can lead to dance!

Birch trees murmur with their laughter,
While sleigh bells echo, ever after.
The hidden wanderer shakes their glee,
Inviting all for winter's spree!

So bundle up and take a chance,
In the crisp air, let's join the dance.
With frozen fingers and frosty cheeks,
The fun of winter is what one seeks!

Frostbitten Legends Awaken

In snowy hills, they start to roam,
With big wooly feet, they feel at home.
They trip on sticks, then tumble down,
With giggles loud, they lose their frown.

Snowball fights turn into a mess,
They throw with force, won't even guess.
When laughter rings, you can't stay mad,
A frosty chill turns just a tad.

Legends whisper from trees so tall,
In furry coats, they heed the call.
They jump and spin like dancing fools,
Who knew the cold could break the rules?

With every howl and frosty shout,
They dance about, there's no doubt.
Whether friend or foe, they claim the snow,
These frosty legends steal the show.

The Cryptic Call of the Ice

The frozen ground begins to hum,
A riddle wrapped in winter's drum.
With fluffy tails and cheeky grins,
They glide and slip, let the fun begin!

A snowman winks, then starts to dance,
In the frosty breeze, they take a chance.
With carrot noses all askew,
It's a snowy party, just for you!

They call to trees with icy breath,
To join the fun, to dodge the theft.
Those cryptic calls echo all around,
And friends emerge from snowy ground.

So, grab your mittens, join the pack,
In a world where fun won't hold back.
With every laugh, the cold's embraced,
Winter's magic cannot be replaced.

Beneath the Frosty Overcoat

Beneath layers of white, a secret stirs,
With giggles and twirls, the magic purrs.
Snowflakes drift by, a soft ballet,
While chubby cheeks grin and sway.

A sleigh rolls past with a joyful cheer,
And fluffy creatures lend an ear.
From beneath the coat of frosty bliss,
Comes a comedic, festive twist!

With ice-skating hippos and penguins, too,
Laughter ignites in the frosty dew.
Each slip and slide, a reason to cluck,
Who knew winter could bring such luck?

But watch your step, the ice might crack,
As these furry friends bounce back.
With every laugh, we celebrate,
In this snowy world, we elevate.

Voices of the Winter's Breath

Whispers ride on crisp, cold air,
With stories spun, oh what a flair!
Snowflakes sing to the icy pines,
In tune with giggles, oh how it shines!

Frozen whispers tease the brave,
Come join the fun, it's what we crave.
From hilltop views, the laughter rolls,
Echoes of joy fill winter's shoals.

They scheme and dream beneath the stars,
Swinging on branches, counting cars.
In the frosty night, they shout with glee,
As winter's breath sets their spirits free.

So gather round, in this snowy embrace,
Let each chuckle be the chase.
For when the winter calls your name,
The funny tales ignite the flame.

The Guardian of the Snowy Vale

In a coat of white so fluffy and bright,
A creature lurks, a comical sight.
With snowball fights and clumsy glee,
He tumbles about like a playful spree.

His laughter echoes, a jolly sound,
As he trips on ice, goes tumbling down.
Atop a hill, he waves with flair,
Who knew a guardian could dance without care?

Snowflakes twirl as he prances around,
A frosty friend that knows no bound.
With a wink and a grin, he leaps with zest,
In the snowy vale, he's surely the best!

So bundle up tight, for joy's in the air,
With a guardian who's happily unaware.
His antics remind us, through laughter and play,
Winter's a party in a snowy ballet.

Unraveling the Winter's Veil

A scarf that's tangled, a hat askew,
He huffs and puffs, 'What shall I do?'
With a tumble and roll, he tries to unwind,
The mysteries of winter, he's determined to find.

In search of warm cocoa, a comedic quest,
He spills the marshmallows, oh what a mess!
With every hot sip, he slurps with delight,
And laughs at the snowflakes that flutter in flight.

A snowman winks, as he trips on a sled,
With a clatter and boom, down the hill he sped.
Through laughter and warmth, he brings us a tale,
Of unraveling myths behind winter's veil.

In the land of frost, where giggles abound,
His cheerful spirit spreads joy all around.
So let us all join in this whimsical game,
For winter's not scary, it's truly a flame!

Twilight in the Frosted Forest

The twilight arrives, with shadows that dance,
A fuzzy creature joins in a frosty prance.
With twinkling lights hanging from each tree,
He spins and he swirls, oh what jubilee!

As hoot owls chuckle, and pinecones drop,
He leaps up high, then makes a big plop.
Whiskered and wide-eyed, he gazes in awe,
At the wonders of dusk, he can hardly draw.

With candy canes tucked in his fuzzy fur,
He munches away, oh what a stir!
As snowflakes swirl and whispers grow bold,
His giggles echo, as the night unfolds.

The moon's silver glimmer, the stars twinkle bright,
In the frosted forest, a joyful sight.
With friends all around, let's revel and play,
For winter's a canvas where laughter leads the way!

The Chill of Untold Stories

Beneath the chill, where secrets are spun,
A creature chuckles, oh what fun!
With tales to share that jiggle and sway,
He gathers the critters to laugh and play.

Around a warm fire, with marshmallows high,
He spins silly stories that make spirits fly.
Of snowmen that dance and reindeer that sing,
Through whimsy and wonders, joy is the fling.

As blankets of white cover land with grace,
He whispers soft fables in this cozy place.
With a twinkle in eye, he leans in close,
To share in the laughter, this winter's boast.

So listen, dear friend, to the chill that stirs,
In the heart of the wild, where laughter occurs.
For stories untold, await in the freeze,
With a giggle and grin, let's savor the tease!

Milton Keynes UK
Ingram Content Group UK Ltd.
UKHW022340171124
451242UK00007B/66